W9-DBE-852

GROWING IDEAS

by

Jean Van Leeuwen

photographs by

David Gavril

Richard C. Owen Publishers, Inc.
Katonah, New York

Meet the Author titles

Verna Aardema   *A Bookworm Who Hatched*
Frank Asch   *One Man Show*
Eve Bunting   *Once Upon a Time*
Lois Ehlert   *Under My Nose*
Jean Fritz   *Surprising Myself*
Paul Goble   *Hau Kola Hello Friend*
Ruth Heller   *Fine Lines*
Lee Bennett Hopkins   *The Writing Bug*
James Howe   *Playing with Words*
Johanna Hurwitz   *A Dream Come True*
Karla Kuskin   *Thoughts, Pictures, and Words*

Jonathan London   *Tell Me a Story*
George Ella Lyon   *A Wordful Child*
Margaret Mahy   *My Mysterious World*
Rafe Martin   *A Storyteller's Story*
Patricia McKissack   *Can You Imagine?*
Patricia Polacco   *Firetalking*
Laurence Pringle   *Nature! Wild and Wonderful*
Cynthia Rylant   *Best Wishes*
Jean Van Leeuwen   *Growing Ideas*
Jane Yolen   *A Letter from Phoenix Farm*

Text copyright © 1998 by Jean Van Leeuwen
Photographs copyright © 1998 by David Gavril

Richard C. Owen Publishers, Inc.
PO Box 585
Katonah, New York 10536

Library of Congress Cataloging-in-Publication Data

Van Leeuwen, Jean.
        Growing Ideas / by Jean Van Leeuwen ; photographs by David Gavril.
            p .   cm . — (Meet the author)
        Summary: The author of the popular books about Oliver and Amanda Pig describes her life, her daily activities, and her creative process, showing how all are intertwined.
            ISBN 1-57274-195-3 (hardcover)
            1. Van Leeuwen, Jean—Biography—Juvenile literature.
        2. Authors, American—20th century—Biography—Juvenile literature.
        3. Children's literature—Authorship— Juvenile literature.
        [1. Van Leeuwen, Jean. 2. Women authors. 3. Authors, American. 4. Women—Biography]
        I. Gavril, David, ill. II. Title. III. Series: Meet the author (Katonah, N.Y.)
        PS3572.A42257G7 1998
        813' .54—dc21
        [B]   98-9372

Editorial, Art, and Production Director   *Janice Boland*
Production Assistants   *Donna Parsons* and *Marc Caroul*
Color separations by Leo P. Callahan Inc., Binghamton, NY

Printed in the United States of America

9 8 7 6 5 4 3 2 1

*For all the children with stories
inside their heads*

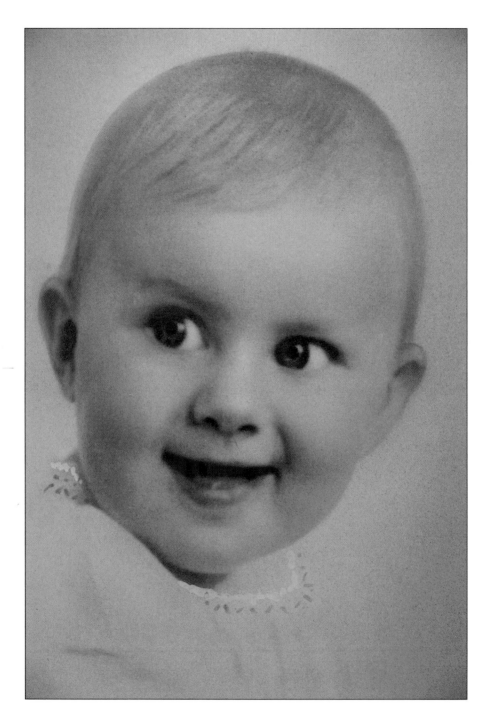

When I was a little girl, I liked to climb trees,
ride bikes, and play baseball.
When I wasn't doing those things,
I was reading. I loved to read books.

For a long time, my favorite books were dog stories.
That was because I desperately wanted a dog.
But my parents wouldn't let me have one,
so I read about them. When I was ten, I finally got
my dog, Cindy. After that, I moved on to horse
stories like *Black Beauty*, then mystery stories.

I read so much it seemed
to me that I had read
every book in the library of
the small New Jersey town
where my younger sister
and brother and I grew up.
So when I was in sixth grade,
I wrote my own book.

It was going to be a wonderful story about a girl
and her horse. I didn't know much about horses,
or about writing a whole book. I got to Chapter 3
and gave up. Writing was too hard, I thought.

Years later, after I graduated from college,
I got a job as an assistant editor in the children's
book department of a publishing company.
There I read lots of manuscripts and books.
After awhile I thought, "Maybe I could write a book."

But this time I wrote about things I knew.
And this time I was successful.
My first published book was *Timothy's Flower*.
It was about a boy trying to plant a flower
on a block like the one I lived on in New York City.

About half the books I have written
were inspired by my own children.
When David and Elizabeth were little,
I started writing down the funny and
interesting things they said and did.

There was the time they put too much bubble bath in the tub, and we had a bubble disaster.
There was David's first day of kindergarten.
There was the "monster bush" in a nearby yard that scared Elizabeth.
Later it became a monster clock in a story I wrote.

Before long, I had a lot of short stories about my family. I called the children in my stories Oliver and Amanda. And because my own children liked books about animals, I decided to make them little pigs. I sent my stories to the editor at the book publishing company that had published my first book. She liked them. And my Oliver and Amanda stories were published.

As they grew up, David and Elizabeth gave me
ideas for books for older readers. I wrote *Benjy
and the Power of Zingies* and *Dear Mom, You're
Ruining My Life*. But they are all grown up now,
so I have to look elsewhere for story ideas.

My ideas come from surprising places.
Something I hear or see or read sticks in my head.
Once I overheard a bunch of nine-year-old boys
talking about horror movies. That became
a chapter in my book *Benjy the Football Hero*.

A sad-looking stuffed rabbit gave me the idea
for my book *Emma Bean*.

And when I was reading a book
about pioneers, one sentence
gave me the idea for a whole story.
I called that book *Going West*.

Each tiny idea grows and grows.
I write notes and put them into a folder.
I ask myself questions like,
"Who are the characters?"
"What are they like?"
"What is going to happen to them?"
"How will the story end?"
Then, one day, magically, I know that it is a story.
And I begin to write.

My work day begins at about nine o'clock.
Right after breakfast, I go downstairs to my office.
I turn on my computer and read over the writing
I did the day before.

I write all morning, and sometimes part
of the afternoon.

Some of my most important writing is rewriting.
I usually write a story over three or four times
before I think it is good enough.

When my brain gets tired, I stop.

If I get stuck on something, I go for a walk. I don't really think about the problem I'm stuck on but as I walk, thoughts pop into my head. By the time my walk is over, a solution has come to me.

In the afternoons, I answer my mail
or talk on the telephone with one of my editors.
And I read. I still love to read.

Some afternoons I work in my garden. Gardening makes me feel peaceful inside.

17

Writing is fun and it's satisfying.
But it can be lonely.
So I like to go out and talk to children.

One afternoon a week I help out in a first-grade class. I work with the children on their writing.

I also visit schools to talk about my books.

I like to work with adults, too.
I have a writing workshop for people
who want to write children's books.
Once a month we meet around my dining room
table. We talk about each person's work
and give suggestions to make it better.

I like to write all kinds of stories
for all ages of children:
funny stories and serious ones;
stories about animals and stories about people;
stories about the past and stories about today.
I enjoy changing from one kind of book to another
so I always have a new and different challenge.
When I'm working on a book about the past,
I need to do research.
I spend lots of time in libraries.
I visit museums and go to historic places.
I want to know all the little details
of how people lived a long time ago.
I look at the clothing they wore
and the cooking pots they used.
I look at old wagons and visit old houses.

For my book *Bound for Oregon*, I went all the way
to Oregon where my story was set and where
my characters traveled on the Oregon Trail.
For another book, I learned how to spin flax,
dye wool, and how to take care of a baby lamb.

My family helps me with my research.
My husband Bruce is a mechanical engineer
and a computer scientist.
He can answer my questions about how things work.

Once he designed a cat trap for one of my
books about mice.

He is usually the first person to read my newest story, even before I send it to my editor.

My daughter Elizabeth helps me remember
the things that happened when she was little.
My son David has given me advice on football
and food fights in the school cafeteria.
He's an artist and a photographer now.
He came back home to Chappaqua, New York
for his father's birthday and took the pictures
for this book.

I think that I am very
lucky. I am doing what
I like best: writing books.

I love taking a blank sheet of paper
and creating a character and a brand-new story
that has never been told before.

Other Books by Jean Van Leeuwen

A Fourth of July on the Plains; Amanda Pig and Her Best Friend Lollipop; Amanda Pig, Schoolgirl; Blue Sky, Butterfly; Oliver and Amanda and the Big Snow; The Girls in Sister Dresses; The Great Summer Camp Catastrophe; Touch the Sky Summer

About the Photographer

David Gavril is a photographer, a writer, and a cartoonist. He lives and works in Boston, Massachusetts. While he was in college, David traveled to Florence, Italy to study art. David's work has appeared in many magazines and other publications. He also wrote and illustrated his mini-comic *Wheelbarrow*. David Gavril is the original Oliver Pig.

Acknowledgments

Photographs on pages 4, 5, 6, 7, 9 (top), and 11 courtesy of Jean Van Leeuwen. Illustration on page 8 from *Timothy's Flower* by Jean Van Leeuwen, Illustrated by Moneta Barnett. Copyright © 1967 by Moneta Barnett. Reprinted by permission of Random House, Inc. Illustrations on page 9 from *Tales of Amanda Pig* by Jean Van Leeuwen, © 1983 by Jean Van Leeuwen. Illustrations © 1983 by Ann Schweninger. Used by permission of Dial Books for Young Readers, a division of Penguin Books USA Inc. Illustrations on page 10 from *Oliver Pig at School* by Jean Van Leeuwen, © 1990 by Jean Van Leeuwen. Illustrations © 1990 by Ann Schweninger. Used by permission of Dial Books for Young Readers, a division of Penguin Books USA Inc. Illustration on page 25 from *Going West* by Jean Van Leeuwen, © 1992 by Jean Van Leeuwen. Illustrations © 1992 by Thomas B. Allen. Used by permission of Dial Books for Young Readers, a division of Penguin Books USA Inc. Illustration on page 27 from *The Great Rescue Operation* by Jean Van Leeuwen, © 1982 by Jean Van Leeuwen. Illustrations. © 1982 by Margot Apple. Used by permission of Dial Books for Young Readers, a division of Penguin Books USA Inc.

J
B

Van Leeuwen, Jean.

VAN LEEUWEN
Growing ideas.